Dying Men

The Broken Divine Order and Downfall of Men

Ka'Vara Jackson

Contents

Acknowledgment III

About the Author IV

Introduction V

1. In the Beginning 1

2. Nature of Sin 8

3. Destruction Then, Destruction Now 22

4. Ezer Kenegdo 29

5. The Grand Plan 39

6. Final Call: Repentance 49

In-text References

Acknowledgments

All acknowledgments go to our glorious God through Jesus Christ who has strengthened and quickened me to manifest His wisdom and work into these pages. I acknowledge, within in my own will, I have not had the slightest idea of ever writing books. Though I count myself to be no author or writer of sort, the Holy Spirit has strengthened me, in my submission to God, to do such. Nonetheless, I am grateful He would grace me with the opportunity to serve Him and fulfill His Will in my life regardless of the greatness of sin I once bore. My life is Your glory, Amen.

About the Author

Ka'Vara Jackson was born in Landstuhl, Germany in 1989 with a father who served in the United States Air Force and a mother who worked in the education field. Getting the opportunity to travel around and experience many different people and cultures, he has had the opportunity to learn and understand many differences. Now serving in the Faith of Jesus Christ since 2014, he has committed and dedicated his life to the Will of God and has been since actively serving and teaching the bible to many, especially those who are new in the Faith.

Ka'Vara is a husband and a father to four young children and currently resides in Houston, TX. His primary focus in his works is to not only ensure his own salvation, but to help lead and encourage others in their own walk of salvation. He prides himself in continuous growth in his personal communion with God through Jesus Christ and constantly searching the Scriptures for reproving and edification.

Introduction

Writing this book has been a Holy Spirit motivated work and solely on the strengths and merits of Jesus Christ, our Lord and Savior. What this book contains is biblical principles, expounding of the Scriptures for further elaboration and understanding of the truth, examples relevant to the subject, and ultimately, a lot of instances of grieving and mourning. The world today is full of imbalances contrary to biblical principles and order with too many different factors being involved. However, what is expressed in truth will resort down to the root of this societal downfall. This book contains hard truths many will not find pleasing, but it is the truth. How true it is the flesh rages war against the Spirit. Therefore, the truth which is within the Spirit of God only hurts as much as the individual is carnal. Coming to understanding of this has increased discerning how much an individual dwells in the flesh by how they respond to the truth.

Now, this book will more heavily deal with men, but this content is not exclusive to men only. Women have a vital role in either the building or the destruction of the man. Today's society is experiencing a decline in men. What is covered here pertains to both men and women, but more emphasis will be on the men. Dear brothers and sisters, all of this is written with absolute love first to our Holy Father and then to all who believe in Him. This book will serve its purpose and bless those whom it is intended for. It is an absolute desire and hope for anyone who reads this, to receive the Spirit of God, be encouraged, and strengthened into full obedience to God, Amen.

<u>In the Beginning</u>

Order of institution from God between man, man and woman, family, state, and church

A look and breakdown founded in Genesis

The history of creation written in the bible will not be so much elaborated here. The six days God worked and the Sabbath on the seventh and so forth is general knowledge today. However, there are some key factors to note in this portion of Genesis which will be focused on. What is deemed to be extremely necessary for any believer, regardless of how mature in Spirit, is to make sure the context of Scriptures is understood from the knowledge and wisdom of God and not man's perspectives or ideas. A well-known statement to date has been proven to be true of how much meanings get lost in translations. Misinterpretations is a dangerous poison to the body of believers, so with great affirmation, be rest assured many specific words in the Scriptures will be pointed out and expounded upon to ensure the meaning of the Text is clear. In expounding the Scriptures and diving into the subject matter, reference notes will be placed at the end of this book for opportunities to obtain additional information. To employ anyone with recommendations on what books to obtain or where to obtain information will not happen. However, above all things, be led and guided by the Holy Spirit as He guides everyone in exactly what is needed according to His divine providences.

Beginning to dive into some key principles, divine establishments, and order of God through the Scriptures, it first must be noted how this area does deal heavily with men. However, this does not mean women do not have a vital role in this. In essence of this, as a woman, find this information to be as equally important to have. The first note is found in Gen 1:26: *Then God said, "Let Us make man in Our image, according to Our likeness; let them have* **dominion**[1] *over the fish of the sea, over the birds of the air, and over the cattle, over all the earth and over every creeping thing that creeps on the earth."* This specific word stated in this Text, dominion, must be understood in accordance with God's wisdom and not according to the doctrines of men. In some translations, this word is substituted with the word rule. According to the Text in the original language however, this word here used is dominion. The first ability God gave men to have was dominion. Dominion specifically was granted to operate and subdue the earth and all its living creatures, which is evidently followed in v. 27-30. The significance is this was gifted to men by God before He even created man. Now, some would argue at this point He had already made both man and woman from the statement in v. 27: *"So God created man in His ow image; in the image of God He created him; male and female He created them."* This idea is obviously refuted in the following Scriptures from Gen 2:18-25. It is imperative to discern and separate the truth in the Word of God from the doctrines of men through the Holy Spirit. It is futile to be consumed in unprofitable discussions and debates on such matters as this. The Word of God is truth, and the Commandments of God are true, and are not to, in no form or fashion, be questioned or debated, but to be only obeyed.

Now, dominion is the first act of God granted to men. Therefore, every man ought to be submitted to this very duty because it is instilled before birth. Men are responsible for exercising Godly management over what He has provided to manage. Nowhere is it written where this very thing is granted unto woman, but this does not mean a woman is exempt, which will be elaborated shortly. To continue further in the next important order and principle, God establishes a dwelling place for Himself and Adam known as the Garden of Eden. Once completed, God placed Adam in the garden and gave him commands found in Gen 2:15-17.

The first major order of establishment here between God and man is **communion**[1]**.** Thus, according to the divine order provided here, all men must first, above all things, establish, build, and maintain a personal dwelling place and communion with God. A typical word spoken more today in place of communion is relationship[a], but there is no evidence of this term used anywhere in the Holy Scriptures. What is written for sure is communion. Nothing should be done above, before, or without this. Everyone should come to understand how humanity is nothing without the One who formed and fashioned them. Therefore, anything performed with His absence is nothing short of worthless. It is essentially an invitation to destruction and amounts to nothing, no matter how much the world attempts to make it seem otherwise. Also consider the nature of Adam communing with God by him hearing the command of God and his act of obedience. What is visible here in Gen 2:16-20 is Adam not debating, arguing, questioning, complaining, nor going back and forth with God. This is an important note in connection to sin and this will be elaborated on later.

The next established divine order of God following communion is **marriage**[2] between man and woman, which is established in Gen 2:21-25. This union was brought forth and ordained by God and Him alone. If any man desires a wife, he desires a good thing because it is the divine nature of God for a man to be joined to his wife. Even so, a man's wife is one whom God has made for him. In essence of this, just as there is no evidence in Scriptures of Adam seeking after a wife, men should not primarily focus on finding a wife. Rather, men should focus on their communion and let God establish the woman fashioned for him. Many of times has Proverbs 18:22 been taken out of context. The Text is true, but the word *finds*[a] is too frequently misused and misunderstood. What makes this so unfortunate is the English language has made way to give the word 'find' at least 35 different meanings and proper interpretation becomes quite challenging in these circumstances. Personal opinions or guesses will not be stated, only what is to be absolute truth. God did not create woman from Adam's rib, place her somewhere randomly in the garden and command Adam to go search for her and establish her as his wife. It is written in Gen 2:22: *Then the rib which the Lord God had taken from man He made into a woman, <u>and He brought her to the man.</u>* If God is the same yesterday, today, and forevermore as the Scripture is popularly quoted, then this order certainly remains true for every man past, present, and future.

What follows the first two establishments is the <u>temptation</u>[1] of the serpent to Even and the sin of Adam, which will be spoken of in more detail later. With this, a significant understanding must be grasped here. The divine order and foundation of communion and marriage were set before the downfall of man through sin. Many have come to not understand the significance in this, which brings heavy grief. These two divine orders set by God, were set in man's purest and most unblemished state. Therefore, communion and marriage are of the highest order established between God and man and should be adhered to with the sincerest reverence to God. Some have ignorantly argued a carnal defense as to why they feel this does not apply to them today. The simple response is they do not comprehend the Will of God. The grand overall scheme, in its simplest form, is to re-establish what was lost in the beginning. In the coming time of this book will there be elaboration of this along with the   effects of sin, but for now, there are still more divine establishments to note.

The next divine order established to man (and woman now) by God is considered more to be a social institution. Specifically, God spoke this command before the coming of marriage and sin. However, it did not take place until after sin. Gen 1:28 states: *Then God blessed them, and God said to them, "Be fruitful and multiply; fill the earth and subdue it; have dominion over the fish of the sea, over the birds of the air, and over every living thing that moves on the earth."* Therefore, the third divine order and the first social institution between God and man is **family**[1]**.** The birthing of this institution is found in Gen 4:1 when Eve gives birth to Cain. Remember, family is based on biological association.

Many have come to know how Abel follows Cain and most are very familiar with what took place between the two brothers. No matter how known it may be, there is another social institution behind Cain's choice leading to his judgment. God implemented a law, or a rule, found in Gen 4:10-15, more specifically in 15: *And the Lord said to him, "Therefore, whoever kills Cain, vengeance shall be taken on him sevenfold." And the Lord set a mark on Cain, lest anyone finding him should kill him.* What is visible here is mankind's first law, or rule, set here outside of the Garden of Eden. This birthed the second social institution established by God to man, which is **state**[2]. Further evidence of this is found five generations down in Cain's lineage through Lamech written in Gen 4:23-24 which states: *Then Lamech said to his wives: "Adah and Zillah, hear my voice; Wives of Lamech, listen to my speech! For I have killed a man for wounding me, even a young man for hurting me. If Cain shall be avenged sevenfold, Then Lamech seventy-sevenfold."* Here, it is very unlikely Cain went around telling everyone he killed his brother and if anyone sees him and kills him because of it, they will be paid sevenfold. Lamech was also born generations later down the road from the time this law was established. This means he was not in existence to be made known of this rule when it was established. Therefore, this was an implemented regional rule made in effect. Remember, state is based on geographical association.

The last social institution established is somewhat of a different case. Everything beforehand was singlehandedly established by God. This last social institution, **church**[1] was established by men and comes two generations down from Adam after Enosh was born. This is found in Gen 4:26: *And as for Seth, to him also a son was born; and he named him Enosh. Then men began to call on the name of the Lord."* Further evidence of this is found in Gen 6:1-2, specifically v. 2 when it says: *that the sons of God saw the daughters of men, that they were beautiful; and they took wives for themselves of all whom they chose.* These men who called on the Lord are here identified as sons of God. A community of people would not be specifically identified as sons of God and not be associated as the church. Remember, church is based on spiritual association. Also note within this Text a reference point and further evidence of what was spoken of about men finding wives for themselves. These men were not focused on their communion with God nor allowing God to bring forth their wife. Henceforth here, these sons of God finding their own wives have been identified with marrying daughters of men, which in the simplest sense, would be identified as the wicked, or sinners.

Many will wonder if all of this is in a logical divine order, then why would the social institution of church be last. What many have come to realize is God works in a supernatural order in many different areas. The overall picture concludes how God first works in individuals before there is somewhat of a gathering of some form or fashion. Scriptures has numerous amounts of evidence of these very same orderly principles throughout the history of man. In relevancy to today and the new covenant, this same order established in the beginning was set in stone by God in a divine way and with purpose. Over the generations however, this has become more and more lost. Today, most men lack the knowledge and understanding of dominion and exercising it, the order of marriage in society has changed drastically, and evil is being embraced at a highly rapid rate. Some would look back ten years ago at the divorce rate and compare it today and say it has improved drastically. The problem with this statement is it is not true. Divorce rates have dropped over the course of ten years because marriage rates have declined over the past 10 years. This means the rate in which society is committing themselves to a covenant marriage now and the rate of divorce is just as much troubling as the high amounts of marriage and divorce rates ten years ago. To pinpoint one specific root issue as to why this is the case would be difficult because there are too many different factors involved. The cause of this impacts not only men, but women also. However, in the sense of all things spirit, a major conclusion is, sin has had a key portion in declining men in society today.

Nature of Sin

The corrupt power that works against the divine order and nature of God

The root to a society of dying men which began in Genesis

Attributes to describe the reason men are dying when they should be rising can be contributed to multiple reasons. They are merely different branches connected to a tree. Even if someone can pinpoint a tree in a forest, they could cut the tree, but it will just grow right back over time. This fact is identifiable throughout the history of men. The question comes to identifying the root of the tree. If anyone were to take the roots of the tree and uproot them, the tree would not only be removed, but it will no longer be able to grow again. This would sever nutrients the roots absorb to grow and survive over a length of time. In the same sense, there is a root within all men and women at work. This force of nature began and entered the world through Adam in the garden. This root is known as **sin**[1] and defines every wicked and evil act taking place in mankind.

Sin has been defined in a broader since today. It is almost completely dismissed and not seen as a problem to God's goodness towards man and woman alike. The works of sin has never been and will never be good because it is against the goodness of God Himself. A specified biblical interpretation of sin can be gathered in Gen 3:17. However, it would benefit none to gather knowledge and wisdom about sin exclusively to one verse when there is much more to gather through v. 1-20. As such, this portion in the Scriptures will be heavily expounded upon to simplify the truth established here. The purpose here is to separate what is truth from the different doctrines of men who preach and teach this Text. This Text will be expounded to clarify what sin is, who has sin, what sin does, and where humanity sits before God in sin.

First, identify what sin is and what Adam has brought forth into the world because of his sin. Many people will teach Eve sinned first because she was first to eat from the tree of knowledge and this is just simply not true. Some teach because she allowed herself to be tempted by the serpent, she committed sin, and this is also not true. To start with understanding the beginning of sin, it entered the world through disobedience. Adam was given a command by God not to eat from the tree of knowledge found in Gen 2:16-17. Notice this command was spoken solely to Adam. In Scriptures, God did not give this very command to Eve. Some will then ask "Well, how did Eve know not to eat from the fruit of the tree then?" The simple answer is Adam told Eve not to eat from the fruit of the tree. Some would argue the Scriptures does not have an account for this statement and it is in fact untrue. This idea stems from the simple principle of a minor lack in knowing God and His ways. He is not man, nor does He operate as man. When God gives a command, it is the same command He gives to anyone else. "Whoever kills Cain, vengeance shall be take on him sevenfold." This rule was put into effect to all and does not have different standards for different individuals. God does not have to give a rule one way to some individuals and then say it differently for others. The standards of God are clear and understandable by all and are without excuse. The specific words spoken by God to Adam concerning the tree in Gen 2:16-17 and the words Eve spoke in Gen 3:23 are different.

To compare the differences between those two portions of Scriptures, God identifies those two specific trees and commands Adam not to eat from one of them, which was <u>the tree of the knowledge of good and evil</u>. Eve does not identify either one of the trees apart from them being *in the midst of the garden*. Here, the Scriptures also shows God telling Adam if he ate the fruit from this specific tree, <u>in that day that you eat of it you shall surely</u>

die. What Eve told the serpent was "God had said, 'You shall not eat it, nor shall you touch it, lest you die.'" God never told Adam he could not touch the fruit, He just told him not to eat the fruit, so where did Eve get this from? Some have even gone further to argue, "how did Eve know they were in the midst of the garden?" The simple answer is because God placed Adam in the midst of the garden when He planted and made every tree grow, including the two specific trees found in Gen 2:8-9. So, to conclude what even Paul speaks to Timothy in 1 Tim 2:14 regarding Adam and Eve is true: *And Adam was not deceived, but the woman being deceived, fell into **transgression**[1]*. It is very important to note how Paul was intentional here in identifying what was done by her specifically as a transgression and only a transgression. Going back to Genesis, it will become clear why Paul identifies what she has done as a transgression. In Gen 3:6-7, when Eve ate the fruit from the tree, The Scriptures shows nothing happened. Following this, when she gave Adam the fruit who was with her at the time, Adam ate it. Once Adam ate the fruit, both of their eyes were opened as a result, and they found themselves to both be naked. Once they heard the sound of the Lord walking in the garden, they hid themselves from the presence of the Lord among the trees. In v.8, God is calling out searching for Adam. There is no account provided here of God ever calling for Eve. They both hid themselves from the presence of the Lord, why is God only calling for Adam? Why is God asking Adam 'where are you' when He knows where Adam is? What is more important is why Adam speaks a thing which God had not permitted him to know. Who said you were naked Adam? God did not say you were naked. You are aware of something now which you were not made to be aware of before. Is this not still a huge problem with man today?

Should this not be considered one of society's mainstream sources of unsound biblical teaching and false doctrines today?

At this point now, a fuller picture of the origin of sin is made clear, connecting all the events leading up to this moment. Not only the beginning of sin is identified here, but also the nature of man ruled by sin and why it opposes the Will of God. Identifying the origin of sin in this Text is best seen in God's judgment upon the serpent, Eve, and Adam. The first judgment was spoken to the serpent in Gen 3:14, which God starts off by saying 'Because you have done this'. Also note the first declaration God made to the serpent is 'You are cursed'. Following this, God pronounces what He will cause to happen to the serpent from then to the end of time. To the woman, here is only established what God will cause to happen until the end of time going forward. Take note of v. 15, specifically the word enmity[a], as this will be elaborated later. Now on to Adam, a judgment summing up what was written in previous Text. God's first statement to Adam was to let him know of his transgression and his disobedience to God's commandment in Gen 3:17. Then God is declaring another curse, but unlike the one directly put on the serpent for what he had done, this one is put on the ground. What follows is God's declaration of what He will cause man to do. Then God concludes by reaffirming His promise to Adam of the consequence for eating of the fruit of the tree, death.

When Adam sinned, death entered the world. Continuing further on down the Scriptures gives more in depth understanding to bring forth this conclusion: *To be in sin is to be absent from the presence of the Lord, and to be absent from the presence of the Lord is death. Therefore, to be in sin is death.* Remember when Adam ate the fruit, their eyes were opened, and they were naked. When they heard the Lord, <u>they hid themselves from His presence</u>. Not only has Adam hid himself from the presence of God, or in short sinned against God, but now he is forced out of the very place God brought him to. This is the very place God brought Adam to have dominion and walk with God. With his disobedience he gave all of it up. As a result, he now lives under the subjective rule of death along with every man and woman born in history except for one person, which will be covered later.

With the origin of sin identified now comes seeing the effects of sin in man both then and today. Looking at Scriptures starting at Gen 3:7, one of the first characteristics is it will cause mankind to know things they were never permitted by God to know. It will also cause man to understand what God has not permitted for man. In curiosity, some dangerously search understanding in what is not meant for man and what happens as a result is shown in what follows. When they knew they were naked they sewed fig leaves together and made coverings, something God had not permitted them to do. To conclude, gaining knowledge and understanding of things man has no business knowing can result in doing things no one has any business doing. Second note of sin is written in v.8. When they heard the Lord walking in the garden, they hid themselves from Him. Sin not only separates man from God, but the working power of sin will cause anyone to hide themselves from God when everyone should be walking and communing with Him. In v.10 Adam's responds to God's voice as being afraid. Being afraid was not so before sin, but obedience was. The next point is found in v.12 when faced with confronting his transgression, Adam's first reaction was to blame his wife. Although it was true Eve ate the fruit and then gave it to him to eat, the nature of sin can cause anyone to project the source of issues onto other people or other things. This is done instead of humbly standing before God and accepting the choices and responsibilities regardless of external factors; sin would have one to strike down others before their own demise. The truth is, Eve did eat and gave to him, but she did not force him to eat, he chose to eat despite. What stopped Adam from reaffirming to Eve not to eat from the tree regardless of what the serpent was saying? Being in sin will lead anyone very far from standing up and accepting their own responsibilities and choices in matters. The commands of God are to simply be obeyed, not to be questioned or debated. Even more, God is all-knowing. Therefore, God does not need anyone to explain or reason things with Him. Simply put, a question God gives anyone requiring a yes or no answer should only be met with such. Anyone who finds themselves to be like Adam in having to explain or reason in response to God's question; this is the working nature of sin at play.

The next question is, 'how is the power of sin at work against the Will of God?' Many answers and examples are written in Scriptures. One of the problems today is the working curiosity of men. They want to conjure up man made wisdom in a desire to have answers and explanations to everything. In one example, an area of this stems in the timeframe between Adam's sin and the commandments God spoke to Moses. Therefore, this will be the area of focus. The primary question asked today is how man sinned against God before all the laws and commands had been established through Moses? A question like this derives from man today still not knowing and understanding the Will of God and what is not God's Will. It is especially grievous considering all humanity has available now compared to the righteous men who stood and lived before Moses time. Consider the righteous and the unrighteous in this timeframe and notice distinct differences in their character and nature. It is visibly seen, in the Scriptures, the difference between those who had the nature of sin at work within them and those who chose the Will of God despite having sin working against them.

The first example of this in Scriptures is Cain and his brother Abel. What is troubling about this story preached today is the assorted doctrines and messages people have managed to summon. To what purpose, maybe a desire in appearing to be someone who has great wisdom and divine revelations? It is not because Cain offered up the fruit of the field in which God did not respect his offering. Certainly, was it not because Abel offered the fat of his firstborn flock while Cain just offered fruit of the land. Should God be limited so much as to be some supernatural being who only accepts certain things from man with some specific underlying requirements? Certainly not! For why should God be reduced to the measuring of men over things He already owns? God is not as much interested in things He already owns as much as He is to bring back into possession, what has willfully decided on its own to walk away from Him. This is the working evidence and doctrine of Scriptures from beginning to end; a creation of God who has decided to walk away from Him, be reconciled back to the love of the One who created it. This is the doctrine of reconciliation and one of the true biblical doctrine of Scriptures. Yes, God would leave the 99 to come searching for the one, being man, who has gone astray from the flock (being the angels, stars, water, dust, trees, wind, and every other single thing God has created) who are still in obedience. What is true in context here concerning God not respecting Cain's offering is Cain's heart and nature. Cain's response to God not respecting his offering was him becoming very angry, resulting in the falling of his countenance established in Gen 4:5. What is extremely magnificent is what God says to Cain in response in V.6,7: *So the Lord said to Cain, "Why are you angry? And why has your countenance fallen? <u>If you do well, will you not be accepted?</u> **<u>And if you do not do well, sin lies at the door. And its desire is for you, but you should rule over it</u>**."* In simplest terms, God is basically saying, 'I am not respecting your offering not because of what you offered, but because there is some underlying work of nature in you which is against My Will. I want you to understand and give you a choice in the matter. I want you to choose Me and My Will and rule over the corrupt nature working against you and I will respect your offerings then.' Many say God gave humanity free will from the beginning. This free will has been taken extremely far away from biblical context. As a result, it has been embedded in people's minds thinking they can do as they please and God is supposed to be ok with it. Biblical free will is the freedom to make a choice between two options. Mankind can either choose God and His Will for their life or can choose to not accept God or His Will. Inasmuch, the choice Cain chose is very clear. As a result, in the end he was ruled over by sin.

On the other side, Adam bore another son named Seth and in his line of descendants was a man named Enoch found in Gen 5:21. He only lived 365 years compared to the others who lived over 900 years. In that time he spent 300 of those years walking with God and did not experience death as a result. Who prefers to walk with God 300 years and never experience death over living three times as long and experiencing death at the end of life? Also, in the beginning of Gen 6, the Scriptures detail Noah and the wicked generation. The big question here is what made Noah different from every other person from his generation? Given in account, the Text established the men in his generation to be deemed wicked in v.5: *Then the Lord saw that the wickedness of man was great in the earth, <u>and that every intent of the thoughts of his heart was **only evil continually**</u>*. This is a precise establishment and meaning of the nature of man who wills against God when it is subjected to the rule of sin. The men of Noah's generation have collectively decided to be against God and His Will constantly every day. They involved themselves continuously in matters which grieves God such as hate, murder, violence, envy, men who were always at odds with one another, thieves, and so forth. This is the condition of these men by the time of the great flood. Noah on the other hand beginning in v.9, is described as just a man claimed perfect in his generations because he simply walked with God. In other words, Noah made a choice to want the Will of God over his own or others around him. When all flesh corrupted their way on earth and filled itself with violence, Noah chose the Will of God. Noah obeyed every instruction and command spoken to him by God concerning the Ark and believed God with everything in the matter of the flood. When the flood was over, he chose to build an alter for the Lord. These are some key notes to take in account in the differences between righteous Noah and the wicked men. In Gen 9, some portions of this Text are very important to also note. First, take note here a re-establishment of God's divine order first established with Adam before sin, dominion specifically. Next, more commands and institution of more laws are established in v.3. Going down to v.6, God establishes a law against the working nature of sin working since Cain. This nature to kill and murder is sin and works against the Will of God. With this rule being established here, man is now without excuse.

Following Noah, the course of man's history begins to cycle again, becoming more and more wicked from generation to generation up until Abram. Abram was a man raised in the house of his father who crafted idols for a living. He decided to leave his father's house in obedience to the voice of God and would go on to become as he is known today. Behind his son Isaac comes two sons, Jacob and Esau. The descendants of these two birthed two nations, Israel and Edom. There are a couple places in Scriptures found in Mal 1:15; Rom 9:13, where it is stated, '*Jacob have I loved, but Esau have I hated.*' With this, the Scriptures gives more in understanding the nature and mind of God towards men.

To begin studying the differences between Jacob and Esau in the events of their lives according to the Scriptures, it is significant to further understand God's desire for man and what pleases Him. Today, such biblical principles are not commonly taught for the simple matter it would oppose the mainstream doctrines such as 'Best Life Now' and the 'Prosperity Movement'. What is even more grieving is if anyone were to ask many, who claim to be believers today, if they prefer biblical truths and the Will of God or teachings on how to live prosperously today, many will choose the ladder and reject the Will of God. What is far worse than this desire of men today is the desire to force this belief on themselves to be the Will of God even when it is not. These doctrines absolutely contradict biblical truths. To conjure up this belief of portraying man-made ideas, throwing His name on it, and worshiping it is idolatry. Much worse is the way in which the term **prosperity**[1] is used today and the truth is, this word is not used one time in all the New Testament. Prosper[a] is used one time in 3 John v.2, prospered[a] found once in 1 Cor 16:2, prospers[a] (or prospereth) is used in the same place as prosper, and prosperous[a] found once in Rom 1:10. Even as much as man has twisted the meaning of this word, what is written in the original Greek Text is the same word used in all those places. In the New Testament, though different forms are written in today's English translation, all have the same meaning.

In the general sense, the differences between Jacob and Esau are very distinct. The man God loved struggled greatly while the man God hated has no record of struggles. In depth, it is safe to conclude Jacob, in the overall course of his life, was beaten half to death while Esau just lived. Many have taught their own ideas why God hated Esau. 'He hated Esau because he sold his birthright for a soup', or because 'he was a hunter while Jacob tended to things at home'. Some have even come to say very craftly how 'he responded to Jacob's deception wrongfully, which brought perpetual feuding between the two nations.' The Scriptures gives a clear answer as to the reason God hated Esau in Heb 12:14-17: *Pursue peace with all people, and holiness, without which no one will see the Lord: looking carefully lest anyone fall short of the grace of God; lest any root of bitterness springing up cause trouble, and by this many become defiled; <u>lest there be any fornicator[1] or profane[2] person like Esau, **who for one morsel of food sold his birthright**</u>. For you know that afterward, when he wanted to inherit the blessing, he was rejected, <u>for he found no place for **repentance[3]**, though he sought it with tears</u>.* Simply put, what is taught about him selling his birthright for morsels is not incorrect teaching, but it is only a portion of the truth. The nature of Esau consuming him in his poor decision, to sell his birthright for morsel, reveals the nature of sin at work in him as a fornicator and profane. Afterwards, he regretted his decision for it. His sorrow was not stemmed from the wrong he committed against God, but because he did not receive his blessing from his father. Therefore, the opportunity to repent before God was absent. instead, Esau was filled with sorrow at the loss of not being blessed and with the anger from his brother stealing his blessing. Thus, a man who refuses to see his wrong before God or repent when they are aware of their wrongs, is a man who is hated by God. David says this best in Psa 5:4-6: *For you are not a God who takes pleasure in wickedness, Nor shall evil dwell with You. The boastful shall not stand in Your sight;* **You hate[1] all workers of iniquity.** *You shall destroy those who speak falsehood;* **The Lord abhors[2] the bloodthirsty and deceitful man**. To summarize in short, God hates those who do wrong. Will anyone find this being taught in the 'Best Life Now' or 'Prosperity' doctrines? Certainly not! For it would render the core of all their teachings to nothing. Yet, many will continue to follow these mainstream teachings. The idea today is pushing God to accept the things He hates while still supplying them with an easy, painless life. In other words, 'to say I want the Will of God in my life according to Scriptures means I would have to give up my idea of living a nice lavish comfortable life. This will result in me not doing the things I want to do'. This is today's philosophical problem amongst many who claim to be in the faith.

  If God hated Esau for this reason, why then did He love Jacob? Jacob deceived Esau for his birthright and then ran off. He sold 14 years of his life to another man because he wanted the younger of his two daughters against traditional customs. Jacob wrestles with God and ends up with a socket in his hip being out of joint. He runs into

Esau later and is in fear Esau is coming to fulfill his desire of killing him after stealing his blessing. Jacob's daughter Dinah gets raped. Two of his sons kill every man in the city and take all the possessions back from the city as a result. His son Joseph is sold into slavery by his brothers and he thought Joseph was dead until his return. He lived his final moments of his life in a famine. These are many examples heard in teachings on Jacob's experiences in his life and there are more. What is written in Scriptures is a mixture of bad decisions and life circumstances outside his control. However, what is certain is none of it would anyone consider to be pleasant experiences. From this perspective, it is easy to say Jacob was not much different then Esau and, in some manner, this is true. both Jacob and Esau made bad decisions. Does God hate a man because of bad decisions? Out of what is written in the Scriptures, more than likely not. What is certain is Esau allowed himself to be subjected to the rule of sin and reject the Will of God. Though Jacob made bad decisions, he desired the Will of God over being subjected to the rule of sin. Evidence is shown on a few accounts between his dispute with Laban, his two meetings with God at Bethel, and his wresting with God to name a few. What is recorded on behalf of Esau's account from all this? He grew wealthy and powerful, lacked nothing, had descendants after him, found a place to settle and live his life. This is a prime example and lesson not to determine God's love or hatred towards humanity based on physical possessions. Rather, if anyone's life resembles closest to Esau, believers should know God's position towards them is the same of Esau. Is this a safe assessment and conclusion to make? Absolutely! God has not changed, does not change, and will never change for anyone or anything. What is established for one is established for all in accordance with His Will and divine providences.

Consider how all of this is applied to men in society today. The answer is simple: mankind wrestles with the nature of sin, which wars against God's Will and nature. This is true for any other man in history and any other man who comes after. These two natures will always be at war within humanity until each one's life is over. In the appointed time, every person will stand before God in judgment and give account for every thought, action, decision, and word ever spoken. The question will not be who lived a perfect life without mistakes, nor will it be on account of a good man or a bad man. In the general sense, does the nature within desire the Will of God like Abram or has it completely been surrendered into subjection to the rule of sin? This will be elaborated further in depth later concerning this matter. Understanding further the divine order of God and the working force of nature against God, how is all this relevant today and how does it contribute to the downfall of men?

Destruction then,
Destruction Now

What began in the beginning still impacts humanity today

If anyone were to research and study some recent cases and gather statistical data on some of the activities happening today, most results are never anything pleasant. To research every living being today on general areas such as marriage and divorce rates, single parents, abortion, and such; the general conclusion is the rates have been increasing over time. However, in the sense of biblical truths, it is already understood those who reject God and have committed themselves totally to the subjective rule of sin have already been judged. Understanding this, believers should come to know, God is dealing with and speaking to those who claim His name and believe they are a part of the body of Christ, especially in the New Testament. As such, just as Scriptures deals with believers, details written here are for those who claim themselves to be believers. It is also for those who may come to desire the Will of God at some point in their life. It would be a great injustice not to identify some key events in recent history and how significant they were in impacting believers and teachings today. More so specifically, events which took place involving those who claimed to be believers or were believers at some point. These events will not be elaborated on too much. With great intent, be encouraged to research and understand the full details personally.

An example of this is the birthing of the conservative Evangelical movement in the early 1900's, which really took a turn with the Scope's trial. Some individuals involved in this matter were believers, possibly believed to be under the Baptist denomination. This trial would initiate a pushed idea of science against religion and religion against science as a result. The evangelical movement also leaned heavily into political matters in this time of history as well. The National Association of

Evangelicals was established in 1942, which is still visible to this day within American government. Also consider and be aware of the decline of 'holistic' clothing from the drastic damages of World War 1. This birthed the movement amongst women known as the freedom of expression beginning in France and the United States. This freedom of expression movement over the course of a century has increased dramatically and has even pushed itself within the walls of believers. There is the World's Parliament of Religions of 1893, where other religions were introduced into America. Then there is also the birthing of the Christian Science movement by Mary Baker Eddy and its impacts on the body today. The NOI was established in American amongst the African American community by W.D Fard in 1930. This is one of many religious events having a large impact on tensions amongst believers to this day. Dennis Bennett is a man believed to be the center of the new wave of charismatic teaching, which began in the 1960's. Bible readings and prayer in the school was deemed unconstitutional around this time as well.

Looking at many people who have turned their backs on the faith and began utilizing God-given talents for the sake of entertainment and fame, there is no one to blame but many who claim to be believers. This is the result of the many bad decisions and choices resulting in what is seen today. To make matters more difficult, many in previous generations have a fixated mindset of what they have and what they are associated to as absolute. There is really no room to question why those who claim to be in the faith, have a hard time reaching the younger generations. In numerous encounters, it is very safe to conclude the younger generation has a heart and a desire for God, but they simply just do not agree with the way

Christianity has become today. Liken it in a sense of a spiritual intuition, if reasonable; something just does not sit right with them. To add to it, why would those who were raised in Christianity grow up and leave to do other things not involving anything in the principles of Scriptures and salvation? Christianity today has become a melting pot of different man-made philosophies, unbiblical man-made doctrines, and teachings. All of it results in the creation and works of idolatry in believers who are completely unaware of such.

What should anyone anticipate and expect from the King of kings of every generation? Though many judge spiritual matters in accordance with what takes place in the world, consider this to be an extremely dangerous approach. Looking at 1 Pet 4:17, Peter begins with the difference between suffering for Christ's sake and others who blaspheme the name. Then he transitions into <u>God's judgment first beginning at the house of God</u>. Yes, where many today who consider themselves to be prophets and those who classify their act as prophecy, mostly tend to have a similar pattern. Often, they are speaking from a response of things visible and translating it to their idea of what is going to happen in the spiritual dimension and ultimately, to the body of Christ. According to Scriptures in 1 Peter, this is backwards. Thus, the Scriptures are fulfilled in Matt 24:3-14 specifically in 11-12: *Then many false prophets will rise up and deceive many. And because lawlessness will abound, the love of many will grow cold.* If anyone were to ask then if God's judgment started in house when He allowed COVID-19, the answer would be no. The reason being is God's judgment begins with revealing to people their sins and transgressions personally or as a collective group together, Then, it is followed by a warning to repent. This is considerably called a grace period today. However, this should be considered and viewed as the closing of God's grace. This is certainly not the beginning of God's judgment, for He has been working to show man's transgressions and sins for quite some time. God is still calling continuously. The time to answer is ever more ending before He truly begins His end work of judgment. In relations to COVID-19, this is not the beginning of it all, nor is it the end of it. The visible conclusion is majority have yet still to answer it. Now with this pandemic, many houses have been forced to close. Many of the unrepented sins behind closed doors have been exposed by the light and made public. Out of sheer desperation for many have they turned to social media and other platforms. These are the very things they once despised and preached against, which they now use in efforts to survive and continue forward. The tragedy of all this is if individuals were to walk up to some of these preachers today and ask them what lesson(s) they have learned from God with the current events. Many answers would be far from what God desires in times like these from what we see in the Scriptures. The grieving part is, if this is the mindset and spiritual position of those who say this is their 'calling', as they say, to lead and teach people to follow Christ, how exactly is this helping men to be true disciples and followers of Christ?

Looking at some warnings written in the Scriptures from 2000 years ago, it is very likely to assess if some of these matters are taking place within the body of believers today. With this, it has become quite clear and evident the conclusion of the current state of men in society today. If the way things have been going continue in its current path, will the result of it point further into destruction? If this holds to be true, then this is not simply of a matter of just accepting for what it is. This mindset has led many people to their demise in times past. If anyone is going to be able to impart any efforts of change, then recognizing and acknowledging things for what they are must come first. Then mankind must have the willingness to fix the error of its ways. Finally, each one must pursue change for the better. Though grace is closing swiftly upon humanity, there is still yet time for everyone to acknowledge, within themselves, their errors and transgressions. Today is the time to no longer subject oneself to the rule of sin and desire the Will of God. This will be further elaborated on later.

To consider what is written in Scriptures concerning the present days, numerous accounts are recorded. Many Scriptures concerning later times have happened or are happening right at this moment. At the same time, some have still yet to be fulfilled. The specific area of Scriptures which will be focused on are more so of what is very identifiable with what is happening now. Some will even be matters which have happened a little time back but are still presently visible to today. In 2 Tim 3:1-9, quite a bit of details is provided, but ones to specifically look at will be noted here. In v.1-4: *But know this, that in the last days perilous times will come: For men will be lovers of themselves, lovers of money, boasters, proud, blasphemers, disobedient to parents, unthankful, unholy, unforgiving, slanderers, without self-control, brutal, despisers of good, traitors, headstrong, haughty, lovers of pleasure rather than lovers of God*. Now remember, be mindful to take these Scriptures in consideration to who it is being addressed to. These Scriptures were being taught to believers, by believers, and the focus was never on the people who are of the world, but of those who considered themselves to be believers. In comparison to teachings today, can anyone say the way in which Scriptures were being taught then are the same now? Further on in V.5-7: *having a form of godliness but denying its power. And from such people turn away! For of this sort are those who creep into households and make captives of gullible women loaded down with sins, led away by various lusts, always learning and never able to come to the knowledge of the truth*. Also continue forward into chapter 4 of the same book at v.3-4: *For the time will come when they will not endure sound doctrine, but according to their own desires, because they have itching ears, they will **heap up for themselves teachers, and they will turn their ears away from the truth, and be turned aside to fables***. Look also into the Scriptures in 1 Tim 4:1-3: *Now the Spirit expressly says that in latter times some will depart from the faith, giving heed to deceiving spirits and doctrines of demons, speaking lies in hypocrisy, having their own conscience seared with a hot iron, **forbidding to marry, and commanding to abstain from foods which God created to be received with thanksgiving by those who believe and know the truth***. Another portion to incorporate is 2 Thes 2:9-12: *The coming of the lawless one is according to the working of Satan, with all power, signs, and lying wonders, and with all unrighteous deception among those who perish, because they did not receive the love of the truth, that they might be saved. And for this reason **God will send them strong delusion, that they should believe the lie***, *that they all may be condemned who did not believe the truth but had pleasure in unrighteousness*.

       There are a few other Scriptures which can be referenced here, but those are mainly some of the clear and precise accounts to be expressed here. If it has become evident and true, different reactions to this reality will come forth. Some will lose all hope and stray from the faith. Some will begin to ponder and think about what they can do differently. There will be some who will know what to do and either do it or not. Then there will be those who do absolutely nothing. Though the events are what they are today, there is still hope as the Scriptures says in Jonah 2:9: ***Salvation is of the Lord***. Also, in 2 Cor 6:2 does it say: **Now is the time of God's favor, now is the day of salvation.** This will be further elaborated on. What has been covered to this moment is the establishment of God's divine order from the beginning, the root cause of declining men, relating what was established from the beginning to today, and the evidence of it all. What comes now is, how are woman involved in all of this?

Ezer Kenegdo

A Suitable Helper

The power to influence in either salvation or destruction in some of the simplest of choices

*I will make him a **helper comparable**[1] to him,* or in another translation, *I will make a **suitable helper**[a] to him.* What this means here is the beginning and purpose of the creation of woman. Eve was made from Adam's rib to be a suitable helper for him. God blessed woman to bear children so the command to be fruitful and multiply could be fulfilled. However, there is something extremely important here about these particular words 'suitable helper'. This frequently misinterpreted Text brought forth several unbiblical ideas of how a woman is to be with man. Out of the many levels of ignorance has humanity initiated some major events shifting the divine order of woman out of proportion. Certain unbiblical philosophies such as women being a lesser person, minimalized, to be a mindless doll who are only allowed to do as one commands, a puppet for one's self-satisfaction and pleasures, or even being identified as a 'trophy' to name a few, have stained and bruised marriages within those who identify themselves to be in the faith. Some movements sparked over the recent century may have begun with good intentions to initiate a better change, such as the feminist movement. The degree of what these movements are today has, in the lightest way put, damaged the order and structure of union designed by God. The ability God has gifted woman is so grand, if submitted to the divine Will of the Father, and performed in a manner pleasing to Him, could produce such monumental results which could shake much of what is happening today. Also, just as much good comes from this, the measure of destruction can equally amount when a woman chooses to not exercise what God has given within the divine order.

Some of the most incorrect descriptions of a woman most often embraced and embedded in this generation is nothing short of troubling. The idea of woman being weak, dependent, needy, vulnerable, or helpless is absolute folly. If this lie is continually embedded in the minds of people, especially those in the faith, the spiritual cap hovering over woman will continually suppress the fullness a woman was made to be. When this spiritual cap remains and compresses the woman from being great, it also compresses the man from being his full potential. To think a woman to be confined as little as making sure a man has a home cooked meal, clean clothes at home, and bearing children is sufficient, men are unbearably deceived. These matters should be a foundational duty of woman, but not considered the grand purpose. Therefore, woman should not be condensed to mere foundational duties when they were made for far greater matters. Even if a man can produce forth any amount of fruit, it would not be anywhere near full potential. So, this term, suitable helper, is not a means of comparison and contrast between woman and man. This means when God created woman, she was created equal to man. If generations of women were not troubled of the idea of being labeled as less equal to man, such movements, like the feminist movement, would probably not exist. Even if it would still exist, more than likely would it be along the lines of doing the same things man can do which. In some areas, it could still be a dangerous matter which will be elaborated later. Suitable helper is not restricted between lines of defined duties and responsibilities. In a general sense, Eve was created to be a fitting addition and help to Adam. So, in the finer essence of it, Eve was able to help increase the fruit of Adam's work, potentially, ten times over than what Adam could do alone. Often is the Text from Deut 32:30 used and misquoted as a reference to emphasize such point. People will generally say "One can chase a thousand and two put ten thousand to flight", but this Text says: *How could one chase a thousand two put a myriad^a to flight, if it were not their Rock that sold them, and Jehovah had shut them up?* In this portion of Scriptures, God here is speaking to Israel concerning the affairs of the nations around them and his burning indignation set forth against them. While it may sound good, taking Scriptures out of context to make a point is a large reason many believers have bad teachings today. If anything is to be gathered out of this portion of Scriptures, it should be a foundational principal expressed all throughout the Bible; no man is able to do or accomplish anything without God. If anyone were to use relatable reference points in the Scriptures, it would be more suitable in pointing to women who are examples. This can include Ruth, Hannah, Esther, Phoebe, Mary, and Elizabeth to name a few.

The idea of woman doing absolutely anything and everything a man commands is futile as well. What is most troubling is the idea of man taking the biblical word submission to justify their unbiblical ways. If man could even, in the simplest of minds, focus on the idea of a woman helping him to accomplish the Will of God and staying on a straight and narrow path, he would be doing ok. For a man to think a woman is supposed to be subjected to any and everything he desires, then he is simply saying he is god, and the woman must worship him. It is a complete tragedy how a man is to lead his wife continually in salvation but brings condemnation upon himself and his wife. Biblical order of submission is best defined in Eph 5:22: *Wives, <u>submit to your **own husbands, as to the Lord**</u>*. Adding to this in v.24 which is more than likely one of the mainstream sources where out-of-context philosophies and bad teachings occur: *Therefore, <u>just as the church is **subject** to Christ, so let the wives **be to their**</u>*

own husbands *in everything*. It is quite a shame for many people to take those last two words in the Text to justify their ways. Man and woman alike, are to submit to everything in Christ and what is commanded in the Scriptures. The husband is the head of the wife just as Christ is the head of the church as stated in v.23. The church is presented to be as the body of Christ. Christ being the head, means the function of the body is controlled by the commands of the head, which is Christ. In other words, the body obeys the commands which comes forth from Christ through the Holy Spirit and the Scriptures. One last important fact to point here is the rest of what v.23 says specifically about Christ which is not spoken of anywhere else between Christ and man: ***and He is the Savior of the body***. This is important because women must always have in mind the difference between man and Christ. Yes, just as Christ is the head of the church, the husband in comparison is head of the wife, but he is not Christ. Christ is infallible, man is fallible; Christ is perfect, man is not; Christ is all-knowing, man is not; Christ is eternal, man is not. Women frequently mistake placing what is of Christ onto a man and always find themselves frustrated or straying from the faith.

As submission is concerned in this matter, submitting to Christ means a woman follows and obeys the commands of Christ and in Scriptures without question or debate. Submitting to this and translating it to the comparison and likeness of the man; this means submitting to the husband is performed if the man is leading in the Will of God according to Christ and the commands in the Scriptures. This also means in everything concerning the value of which the husband holds, the woman must also be equal to it and never extend beyond or over it. For example, A command written in Scriptures is to submit to government found in Rom 13. If government tells believers to denounce Jesus Christ as Lord and Savior, should they submit to it? Absolutely not! To obey anything which is contrary to Scriptures would be to disobey God. This would conclude man continuing to be disobedient and in sin. If the man says, 'I will not denounce Christ', but the woman says she will because governing authorities asked, she would then be overstepping her place in accordance to divine order. There is also submission even to unjust government and a command to pray for governing authorities. Even with being married to an unbelieving husband, there is still a command to submit. The overall grand purpose of it is to exemplify the glory of God's goodness through obedience. This can open potential possibilities for the heart and ways of a man to be turned by the Spirit of God.

A good example of this is a strong devoted woman to the works and ministry within her fellowship who has an unbelieving husband. She is there for every event and meeting faithfully and she spends a significant time serving. One day the unbelieving husband gets upset and complains how she spends so much time in her meetings and not enough time at home. His major complaint is how some stuff at home is not being done. The woman responds by letting him know how she understands and will agree to take some time out from some of her meetings as long as she can continue to attend the Sunday and midweek meeting. The husband agrees, the changes are implemented, and both are satisfied. Some will say it is not the Will of God for someone to commit less or devote less than what they are already doing, but this philosophy is not sound. Would God be able to move upon the heart of the unbeliever when she is submitted to God and His commands, but disrespects her unbelieving husband? The possibility is greater for an unbelieving husband to grow furious with his wife and angry at God. This is because she prefers to neglect her duties at home by consuming all her time in the work of ministry. Nothing exceeds submitting to Christ. Submitting to the husband is to obey everything which is in subjection to the Will of God and the obedience of Scriptures. In a simple picture, if the husband says he would like for the woman start praying before starting anything new in the day, she would do well to obey these instructions. If the husband asks for her to go sell herself off so he could become rich fast, to obey such would disobey God and the Scriptures, so a woman would do well not to subject herself to anything of the sort. Whatever is outside of this is unbiblical and an error of man's ways contrary to the Scriptures.

If a woman can help a man become significantly much greater, then is it possible for a woman to also destroy a man? Certainly! It can be just as easy to help destroy a man as it is to help build him further. If it has not been taught or made clear how powerful this matter is, numerous amounts of Scriptures speak of this matter. There are plenty of women in the bible who are prime examples of such. In Prov 14:1: *The wise woman builds her house, but the foolish pulls it down with her hands*; Prov 21:19: *Better to dwell in the wilderness, than with a contentious and angry woman*. Take note the symbolism of the desert to represent a desolate place. This is a symbolic representation considered to be the dwelling place of demons. In other words, it is better for a man to be in a desolate place surrounded by a bunch of demons than to live with a woman who is angry and quarrels. Prov 25:24: *It is better to dwell in a corner of a housetop, than in a house shared with a contentious woman*. Prov 21:9: *Better to dwell in a corner of a housetop, than in a house shared with a contentious woman*. Anything the Scriptures tells more than once; it is a must to know what is written is of huge significance. Prov 12:4: *An <u>excellent wife</u> is the <u>crown of her husband</u>, but she who <u>causes shame</u> is like <u>rottenness in his bones</u>*. Prov 27:15: *A <u>continual dripping on a very rainy day</u> and a <u>contentious woman are alike</u>*. The initial soft continuous dripping sound quickly becomes irritating, frustrating, aggravating, or worse, driving quick response to stop or rid the noise. Prov 31:30: *Charm is deceitful and beauty is passing, but a <u>woman who fears the Lord, she shall be praised</u>*. Some notable examples in Scriptures would be Jezebel, Delilah, Peninnah, and Job's wife to name a few. In context of the details here, Jezebel would be of the greatest example in most, if not all, areas.

Now, to translate this into the New covenant, more specific details and commands to woman are provided here, helping make more areas clear. However, there are some which have been used to justify man's errors and unbiblical mindsets. Generally, what is written in the New Testament contains more details on living and conducting oneself in holistic living, all which pleases the Father. A good example of such is found in 1 Tim 2:9-12: *In like manner also, that the women adorn themselves in modest apparel, with propriety and moderation, not with braided hair or gold or pearls or costly clothing, but which is proper for women professing godliness, with good works. <u>Let a woman learn in silence[a] with all submission. And I do not permit a woman to teach or to have authority over a man, but to be in silence</u>*. This Text has some specific details regarding conduct, but a portion of this Text is highly debated and misinterpreted concerning a woman being in silence. In the matters of God's divine order and Will, the focus is not to be emphasized on learning in silence, but what follows, doing so with all submission. As a woman, it is good to take note of such and apply. Specifically in marriage, it has been made clear of why this is vital. Looking at 1 Cor 14, Paul explicitly emphasizes order in the way matters are to be done and conducted in v.26-39. Inasmuch, in v. 34-38 Paul is speaking of order concerning woman: _Let your women keep silent in the churches, for they are not permitted to speak; but they are to be submissive, as the law also says_. _And if they want to learn something, let them ask their own husbands at home; for it is shameful for women to speak in church. Or did the word of God come originally from you? Or was it you only that it reached?_ **_If anyone thinks himself to be a prophet or spiritual, let him acknowledge that the things which I write to you are the commandments of the Lord_**. _But if anyone is ignorant, let him be ignorant._ Many will say this is very strong or harsh, and some will dangerously challenge the Scriptures concerning this matter. Nevertheless, as Paul states, it is a commandment. Just as important as being a commandment, it is of order. A man, in his duty, ought to be teaching and leading his wife and family in the Will of the God and through the Scriptures. How much more will he be fulfilling such a great duty if his wife, aligned in the order of the Scriptures, seeks her husband in learning of God in the Scriptures? The disappointing part in this is, most people today focus and debate on the emphasis of a woman being silent and women preaching.

Does this mean women are not permitted to speak or teach anything? Absolutely not! Just because Paul says it is not permitted for a woman to teach or exercise authority over a man does not mean a woman cannot teach or exercise any authority. He is simply and specifically referring a woman to a man. The next question is, who can women teach? Women can teach other women and children. Paul specifically mentions for a woman to be silent within the assemblies but take note these are assemblies in which men are present. This does not restrict for women to get together and teach one another. In fact, Paul exhorts and commands such in Tit 2:3-5: *The older women likewise, that they be reverent in behavior, not slanderers, not given to much wine, **teachers of good things** – that they **admonish**[1] the young women to love their husbands, to love their children, to be discreet, chaste, homemakers, good, **obedient to their own husbands, that the word of God may not be blasphemed***. In short, 'Titus, teach the older woman to set an example for the younger women. Have them teach the younger women these duties for the sole purpose of God's divine order so His name will not be blasphemed. Many who are focused on a woman being silent will find what Paul says to be harsh and a problem today in society, especially those heavily influenced by some of these mainstream movements. However, if anyone is focused on the divine order and glory of God; if man continues not to acknowledge this or teach this in their home, as Paul states, it is in ignorance. Any woman who acknowledges this and applies such will be further pushing their husbands in greatness. While the world says women should be pastors and preach in gatherings, choose which is more important. Is it more important to have a platform and a name known amongst many, or is the glory of God more important? Is it more important to be above the man or with him? Is it better to rise above man or to rise with man? For anyone who chooses the glory of God above all else, they do well. As such, also anticipate the offenses, which will follow from men and women alike. Do not allow it to be a stumbling block meant to hinder total obedience and turn one from the faith. Light has no fellowship with dark nor does the dark have any fellowship with light. Not only do they have no fellowship with one another, opposing forces can not agree. Always be in reminder of such and be encouraged.

The Grand Plan

Identifying the purpose in God's work

On the account of Luke, he states something in Scriptures not found on the account of Matthew. Specifically, Jesus gives a few parables to Pharisees who are talking amongst themselves of how He eats and receives sinners. The parable of the 99 and the one lost sheep is used in many different reasons. Some would use it as a means of encouragement for witnessing, or to not let a brother or sister, who may be struggling in the faith, drift off or be alone. Though these may be philosophically reasonable, Jesus gives more than the parable of the lost sheep in what He is teaching. In different examples of the lost sheep, the woman losing a coin, and the parable of what is known to be the prodigal son, Jesus derives to the same result in all of them. There is a huge reason why Jesus, though He is speaking different scenarios, is expressing the same result. Look at the joy filling heaven when something, which is deemed lost, is found again. While Jesus did share these parables in response to the Pharisees murmur, the whole purpose was not simply a response to their murmur, but a means to reveal something important the Pharisees still refused to understand. In Luke 15:7 Jesus says: *I say unto you, that likewise joy shall be in heaven over one sinner that repents, more than over ninety and nine just person, which need no repentance*. Heaven will be filled with joy over the one which has come to be restored back to the Father. Man has made a choice to disobey and walk away from the One who created them. Even still, God is also giving mankind the choice in coming back into right obedience and communion with him.

In the multiple works performed by God throughout the history of man from Cain to Noah, to Abram, Isaac, and Jacob, to Moses and Exodus, the conquest of Joshua and Caleb, to King David and Solomon, and so forth down the timeline, mankind has walked away from God. However, His love has always continued to pursue, especially anyone who would desire Him. Even in the times when hope for humanity seemed lost entirely, it did not stop God from continuing to reach out and call man back. If anyone questions then, why God will continue to reach out to a creation still willing to disobey him; heaven is filled with joy even if it is just one person who decides to return to the Father. Even so, there is more specifics in God's desire with man, which can be identified from the beginning of history. It is very well-known what believers know today concerning Adam and the garden but consider this: Take some time to understand the significance of God having a dwelling place on earth amongst His creation. Understand why God continuously fights and works to be able to dwell with man on earth.

Since being kicked out of the garden, the next major place in history is found in Exodus. God was leading the people Israel, seen as a cloud by day and a pillar of fire by night, stated in Exo 13:21. Now the place where Israel would come to dwell Is extremely important. The nation of Israel is at the center of the region's most political, military, and financial powers who were constantly at odds with one another. In Psa 83:1-8, <u>ten nations</u> are listed here who have risen to conspire against the nation of Israel. These nations surrounding Israel includes Tyre and Gebal to the north (region of Lebanon), Philistines and Amalek (Egypt region) to the west, Edom and Ishmaelites to the southern area (Saudi Arabia region), Moab, Ammon, and Hagarenes (Hagrites) to the east (Jordan region), and the Assyrians (Assur) to the Northeast and further east (Syria and Iraq regions, possibly even parts of the Iran region). Some wonder why God would take a nation, He made clear was fewer in number and weaker than the others and place them in the center of a region surrounded by threats. Some would say God desired to have Israel drive out other idolatrous nation. Though this may be partly right, it is not the whole picture of God's Divine Purpose. God speaks in Eze 18:23: *Have I any pleasure at all that the wicked should die? saith the Lord God: and not that he should return from his ways, and live?* Again in 2 Pet 3:9 it is written: *The Lord is not slack concerning His promise, as some men count slackness; but is longsuffering toward us, not willing that any should perish, but that all should come to repentance.* Once established in the land God promised, numerous accounts of battles take place. God being involved in them with His people occur all the way up to the time of Solomon. This is another instance and clear picture of God's grand plan. In the time of Solomon, the building and establishing of the Temple of God takes place. This temple is the place which God would dwell amongst His people. It is written in 1 Kin 9:3: *And the Lord said unto him, I have heard thy prayer and thy supplication, that thou hast made before me: I have hallowed[1] this house, which thou hast built, to put my name there forever; and mine eyes and mine heart shall be there perpetually.* More evidence is provided here of God's continuous efforts to dwell with His people. To give a clear answer as to why God would put a smaller nation at the center of a power struggle between surrounding nations; this portion of Scriptures makes it clear. Surrounding nations are filled with idolatrous practices. The root of the quarrels consist of who's god(s) are stronger and better. Now Israel comes into the picture saying their God is the living God and the God of hosts. These surrounding nations are looking at their size, strength, and power and they conclude by mocking them and their God. However, when they are confronted in battle, they are baffled at how a weak and small nation could be so powerful to withstand them. Maybe the God of Israel is the real living, most powerful God of all gods. Now, Solomon builds this spectacular temple. He is well-known amongst the nations for his work, wisdom, and wealth. What could possibly be the result of the posture of the surrounding nations? Henceforth, we see people now coming in from all different directions into Jerusalem to meet this king Solomon and the mighty God who rules them. So, the picture of God's influence, and the people's obedience to Him, resulted in people from other religions and gods to come and know the one true living God. Therefore, at the center of Israel would God's glory manifest and result in seeing a lost creation return to Him. Though the Will is visible, one problem was initiated through Solomon. This led to a multitude of problems for Israel (and later Judah). Ultimately, it would lead God in having to work again for the very people He had set apart from the rest. At times, some would repent and obey God, but most of history is filled with disobedience and idolatry.

If anyone were to wonder if God would do again what He did in the days of Noah, it would be reasonable. However, God made a covenant with Noah He would never flood the earth again and the rainbow is a sign of His covenant. Coming forth beyond the days of Solomon, is God continuously working for an idolatrous, unbelieving nation to repent and be restored. Many would look at instances God performs judgment upon Israel, and surrounding nations, and wonder why He punishes man to the degree He does. People fail to realize one very important thing: God performs so all humanity can see Him in It all, believe who He is, and have a desire to commune with Him. In generally most, if not all, acts God performs, He does make known a reason for doing what

He does by simply saying "And they shall know that I am the Lord". For some time, God has been speaking and warning nations. He does not simply say He is going to bring about destruction because the nation is doing something He does not like. Through an extension of mercy and grace, He warns first. Multiple accounts in Scriptures provide evidence when God would speak to a nation, letting them know of their activities. This can include physical activities such as murder, robbing the poor, or neglecting the widows to name a few. God also speaks to the people according to the conditions of their hearts and their mindsets. One example of this can be found in Eze 12, when God spoke warnings to Israel in their time of captivity because of their rebellion. One of the sayings, or proverbs, of the people in these times found in v.22 was, '*the days are prolonged, and every vision fails.*' The mindset of the people here in v.*27 was: "Son of man, look, the house of Israel is saying, 'The vision that He sees is for many days from now, and He prophesies of times far off.*' God responds to it in v.28 when He says: *Therefore say to them, 'Thus says the Lord God: "None of My words will be postponed any more, but the word which I speak will be done," says the Lord God.*'

Over the course of historical timeline, Scriptures record generations and kings who obeyed and pleased God and those who did not. As more time passed however, mankind continued to spiral down. Men and women were getting worse in sin and the desire to commune and obey the commands of God grew weaker. The last book and prophet in the Old Testament, Malachi, gives detailed descriptions of God's position towards His people before there is an absence of recorded Scriptures leading to the New Testament. Mal 3:8-12 is a mainstream reference today in tithing and offering messages, but it is one of many times God is revealing the error of the priests and people in those times. God also speaks of the level of infidelity, the complaints of the people, polluted offerings, and how the nation of Israel questioned and doubted God's love for them. The gap of time here between Malachi and the New Testament is 400 years and many are curious as to what could have happened in this amount of time. The truth is a lot happened with Israel and it would be a great benefit to research and learn what happened in those times. A lot of what is provided in the New Testament with the religious political groups and the important figures around the time of Jesus will become clearer. Jumping into what is written in the New Testament without details of the 400-year period is like attempting to begin watching a movie from the middle.

At this point in time, it would be reasonable to believe God would begin again with mankind similar in the days of Noah. However, He has been prophetically speaking His Will and plan through His Prophets over many centuries leading to this date. Thankfully, what God has spoken then has become more enlightened to mankind today. Ultimately, what was to come has come to pass. In the greatest time of darkness upon the earth, a great light was born. In essence, instead of having another act of wiping man from earth and maybe sparing a few righteous individuals to start anew, God does something different by sending His own Son into the world. Paul says it best in 2 Cor 5:21: *For He made Him who knew no sin to be sin for us, that we might become the righteousness of God in Him.* Yes, this may be a wide scale controversial discussion and, at times, debate today on this man, Jesus Christ. Many question and challenge the validity of His existence, His authority, and even if He is what the Scriptures says He is. For the sake of the simplicity of the grand plan of God and to erase all these different man-made philosophies and ideas, looking solely from the perspective of God alone and the position of mankind before Him, there simply is not any room to question or challenge who He is. Rather than accepting the fact all mankind has sinned before God and deserves eternal death in God's righteous judgment, generations today have been blinded to the truth of where they stand before God. Too many attempt to use Jesus as a fuel for their racial, anti-religious, God-denying behaviors and arguments. All of this is simply mankind finding new ways to justify in refusing to repent and commune with God. Humanity is forgetting more, what Christ endured leading to the cross, is but a small portion of the punishment everyone honestly deserves.

In considering the law and the commands established through Moses, every man and woman has fallen short. To put hope in one's own ability to please God through obeying the commands puts all men and women short and pending judgment of eternal death. Ultimately, who has any room to question if God extended a greater means of grace and mercy by sending someone? He not only took the punishment man deserves, but also gives hope in being able to live a life reconciled back to the Father while walking in a way which pleases Him. Every man has one life to live, and how each one chooses to live and believe before God is each one's own choice. Westernized free will has poisoned people severely. How dangerous a thought for anyone to think they can live life as they please until they believe they are ready to come to God or before they feel life is at its end? Even if anyone is fortunate to have such an opportunity, who can say they will still enter the Kingdom of heaven? The New Testament letters, from Romans to Revelations, gives numerous accounts of distinct and specific descriptions separating those who will be with God and those who will not come judgment day. One such example in Rom 8:9: *But you are not in the flesh but in the Spirit, if indeed the Spirit of God dwells in you.* <u>*Now if anyone does not have the Spirit of Christ, he is not His.*</u> Ultimately, no man should involve themselves in judging whether a person has ascended into heaven or descended into eternal darkness. However, everyone should evaluate their own life according to the Scriptures. If any man would spend more time focused in where he stands before God daily, man would spend less time debating and quarreling on unfruitful matters.

This is the free will provided to man; though man has decided to walk away from God in disobedience, and have now since recognized the error, whosoever desires and chooses to be reconciled back to the Father shall experience life and be saved from the condemnation. Whosoever chooses to continue in disobedience to God shall ever more continue in the path of everlasting death. This is the choice man has been gifted since the fall of Adam. The idea of free will in western culture today is nothing short of destructive. Having anyone to think life is about living how one pleases and knowingly living an unrepentant lifestyle is an extreme risk and threat to one's hope at eternal life. This destructive philosophy has bled into the body of those who claim to be believers. A matter such as this has blinded many in the error of their ways. Many do not realize they have created an idolized god, believing they can live and be any kind of way and this 'god' is supposed to accept it no matter what. What is really being put in God's face is man telling God He should quit working to reconcile and transform the nature of man from sin to the life-giving Spirit, change who He is, and accept humanity with the very things He despises. The reality is, God will never change. He will always love righteousness and abhor evil, love good and hate sin, and welcome anyone who desires to be with Him.

Another troubling matter is the number of individuals who desire to disregard the New covenant grace extended to mankind for the sake of religion and Old covenant law. If man were able to walk in every command without breaking one, there would have not been a need for a mediator nor the Holy Spirit to strengthen mankind in obedience. In general, what is being stated before God is this: they have no need for God's aid in helping them to live according to the law, as if they are greater and better than those who were not under the covenant of grace. Even on what may appear to be the best of days, in the eyes of God is man still visibly filthy rags before Him. Paul says this best in Rom 8:3,4: *For what the law could not do in that it was weak through the flesh, God did by sending His own Son in the likeness of sinful flesh, on account of sin: He condemned sin in the flesh, that the righteous requirement of the law might be fulfilled in us who do not walk according to the flesh but according to the Spirit.* Now, Paul here is not saying the law of God was weak nor is he saying he did not strive to walk according to the law. What Paul realized and is speaking of here is this: though he desired to obey God through the commands, he found the flesh to be too weak to fully obey the commands of God in a way which pleases Him. As a result, He sent Christ, who knew no sin, to condemn sin the flesh, which has now been done where the righteousness in fulfilling the law now abides within those who receive Him. This now gives anyone the ability and strength to overcome the desires of the flesh and to walk in righteousness, which man is unable to do on its own. As if man telling God they do not want Him is bad enough. God has freely given man a gift and supernatural help. This gift solidifies true believers as children of God and transforms the nature to conform to righteousness, which is known as being '<u>born again</u>[a]'. For humanity to have the audacity to respond by saying, 'no need for this either', is a very unfortunate folly of mankind.

What makes the New Covenant so spectacular in conjunction to God's grand plan is how God dwelling with His people is no longer tangible to one specific and collective nation. Now, the Spirit of God resides in everyone who receives and communes with Him. From the time of God and Adam in the garden, to the days of Israel in Exodus, further down the road to David and Solomon and the temple, In the few instances of Israel's captivities to the birth of Christ, and beyond the cross of Christ to the gift of the Holy Spirit; this is such a marvelous work and picture of God always working to dwell with man. In spite of the countless times mankind has chosen to walk away from Him, He has continued to extend His love with open arms. Such glory in God who has done supernatural works through Christ, beyond human comprehension. What began with dwelling with one man and woman to then dwelling with one nation, has now become the Spirit of God dwelling within each individual. Any individual is now able to have their own personal dwelling place with God as He has now made a dwelling place within man. As extravagant as this is, the truth is, God does not simply dwell in anyone or anything. The final question now becomes, how can an individual be someone in whom God dwells within and how does one have the assurance of it?

Final Call: Repentance

The work of man in being reconciled back to God

Many are called, but few are chosen. This Text is quoted too many times to count, but what does it mean? Some will answer and say 'purpose'. Purpose is a little bit of a tangible answer, but when many are asked to be more specific, many equate it to some sort of calling into ministry or work for God. To take this answer and compare it to the context of the Scriptures is nothing short of a complete misunderstanding to the true nature of God's calling upon humanity. This portion of Scripture quoted is found in Matt 22:14. However, v.14 is in conjunction to the parable Jesus is giving beginning in v.2 of the chapter. Looking at v.2-3, it is written: *"The kingdom of heaven is like a certain king who arranged a marriage for his son, and sent out his servants to call those who were invited to the wedding; and they were not willing to come."* Jesus begins the parable, along with others, by giving a picture of heaven. These two verses, while testifying of what is to come, it also slightly gives a picture between humanity and God in the beginning. This Text could also be a picture of Christ speaking of the transition from the old covenant to the new. God sent out *his servants to call those who were invited to the wedding* can be God sending out His servants, the prophets, to call His people, Israel, to be a welcomed guest in a special ceremony. Then the result of the invitation is, *they were not willing to come.* In v.4-5 is a repeat of the preceding verses with more details. It is written: *"Again, he sent out other servants, saying, 'Tell those who are invited, "See, I have prepared my dinner; my oxen and fatted cattle are killed, and all things are ready. Come to the wedding."' But they made light of it and went their ways, one to his own farm, another to his business."* Not only is God extending an invitation to be guests at a ceremony, but He goes further on to tell them of the extravagant meal He has already prepared for them. Yet, the guests respond by preferring to go back to their own places and ways rather than be partakers of something extraordinary and beyond anything humanity has ever experienced. Some of the guests preferred to go back to their own farms and businesses than to be fellow partakers of a once in a lifetime event. Much more in v.6 the rest of the invited guests decided to do something worse rather than attend the ceremony. It is written: *"And the rest seized his servants, treated them <u>spitefully</u>^a, and killed them."* Indeed, does the picture seem to be more of a representation of God and the nation Israel.

After v.6, a reaction from God concerning the guests' rejection and response to the invitations is noted here. In v.7-8 it is written: *"But when the king heard about it, he was furious. And he sent out his armies, destroyed those murderers, and burned up their **city**. Then he said to his servants, 'The wedding is ready, but those who were invited were not worthy.'"* God became angry with the invited guests and the result of it is here established. These invited guests were identified to be murderers and God set armies to destroy them and burn their city. Once, a special group of people, are now noted here as 'not worthy'. In v.9 the Scripture says: *"'Therefore go into the **highways**, and as many as you find, invite to the wedding.'"* With this, it is very probable to potentially compare this with the beginning of God's new work done in the new covenant. Something specific and certain within the symbolism of this Text is provided here. To say in part, if Jesus is revealing the grand plan of God in a parable to the Sadducees, then it is extremely likely the invited guests, who God sent armies to destroy and the city to burn, is a representation of the nation of Israel. Now God is extending invitations to anyone spotted on the highways. These highways are located outside the city, which would very likely be a representation of the Gentiles, or those not original partakers of the commonwealth. To conclude this portion of the parable to signify the beginning work of the new covenant within its symbolism would be very considerable. Now looking in v.10 it is written: *"So those servants went out into the highways and gathered together all whom they found, <u>both bad and good</u>. And the wedding hall was filled with guests."* One thing must be cleared here. Is Jesus saying good and bad people were able to attend the ceremony? The answer is yes and no. The yes portion of this question is understanding something very important. The invited guests in the wedding ceremony are not based on a mixture of good and bad people after the fact. Even though gentiles were excluded from the commonwealth initially, there were still good people. In fact, many works and miracles God performed before the time of Christ involved Gentiles. Even in the time of Christ, a lot of significant miracles recorded were performed on Gentiles as well. If any man concludes he can be a bad person and still be a guest in the ceremony, he is deceived. What this does mean is anyone is able to come to the Father regardless of the life or lifestyle everyone has lived. Through His servants, He has extended an invitation to anyone they see on the highway and look at the difference in results; *the wedding hall was **filled** with guests.*

Now, looking at v.11-14, what Jesus speaks to the Sadducees gets very interesting. The Scriptures say: *"But when the king came in to see the guests, he saw a man there who did not have on a wedding garment. So he said to him, '<u>Friend</u>, how did you come in here <u>without a wedding garment</u>?' And <u>he was speechless</u>. Then the king said to the servants, 'Bind him hand and foot, take him away, and <u>cast him into outer darkness</u>; there will be* *weeping and gnashing of teeth.'* **<u>For many are called, but few are chosen.</u>"** After God comes in to see all the guests, He notices one who stood out from the rest. This individual was not wearing a wedding garment. A couple notes to take here concerning this individual is the position, location, and encounter. The position of this individual is he found his way into the courts of God's people. Let this be a reminder to ministers. Not everyone who comes in the crowd will have a true heart for God. Notice this individual is inside the wedding hall, in the kingdom of heaven. When God approaches Him, interestingly, He identifies him by calling the individual a <u>friend</u>. This non-wearing garment figure is more significant than those who chose to reject the invitation to the wedding but is not enough to be a continued guest. This is more than likely a symbolic evidence of those who come to fellowships and gatherings for any reason except having a pure communion with God. Even in heaven there is a gate leading to eternal darkness and not everyone is safe from being casted into it. Would be but a complete shame and disaster to enter the gates of heaven and still end up in the gates of Hades. The man's response to God's question was he was speechless. Anyone who has a true heart for God will not sit speechless when approached by Him. Any true saint has come to realize the error of their ways and what they deserve for it, but in a cry for mercy and forgiveness have they obtained mercy from God and have been cleansed with hyssop, or in the covenant of grace, with the blood of Christ. After everything was said and done, the man was cast into the outer darkness for eternity. Then Jesus concludes the parable by saying *'For many are called, but few are chosen'*. Although many like to equate this Text to mean a 'purpose' or 'assignment' or 'chosen for some type of ministry or position', this is simply not what Jesus was speaking here in this parable. God is always more concerned with the soul of a person than He is the titles. More so, these ideas would be more equated to God's plan for each person rather than His call.

What separates the called and the chosen? What separates those who are to be partakers of the ceremony and those who will be cast into the outer darkness? Those who are chosen will be any who have willingly accepted the call to **repentance**, received the Holy Spirit of God, and obeyed the commands of God written in Scriptures. The many who are called but not of the chosen few are simply those with an unregenerate heart. Simply put, those who chose not to obey and accept the call to repentance. Repentance has been a call by God centuries before the new covenant and was not even limited to Israel. He has called Nineveh into repentance in the time of Jonah, and they answered it for example. Esau, as an example stated earlier, is a prime example of an unrepentant person. Where God stood with him as a result, has been clearly stated. In fact, every nation has all received the call for repentance. Also consider Jesus using the specific word 'many' and not 'all'. Does this mean there are some who never receive the call? Absolutely! The Scriptures have specific details of those who do not receive the call.

In the beginning, a note was mentioned on the specific word enmity[1]. There is enmity between woman and serpent, the nations of Israel and Edom who are descendants of Jacob and Esau, some nations are at enmity with one another still to this day, and there is also enmity between man and God through sin. This is not to be compared to enemy. Though an enemy will be at opposition, there is still room for reconciliation between the two opposing forces. Even Jesus gives a command to love enemies in Matt 5:43-44: *"You have heard that it was* said, *'You shall love your neighbor and hate your enemy.'* *But I say to you, <u>love your enemies, bless those who curse you, do good to those who hate you, and pray for those who spitefully use you and persecute you.</u>"* However, the one at enmity with God, there is no hope or chance of reconciliation because these individuals have surrendered themselves in complete subjection to the flesh and will never repent. There is a perpetual hatred in these individuals towards God. Paul says this best in Rom 8:7: *Because <u>the carnal mind is enmity against God; for it is not subject to the law of God, nor indeed can be</u>.* James elaborates further in Jam 4:4 by saying: *Adulterers and adulteresses! Do you not know that <u>friendship with the world is enmity with God</u>? Whoever therefore <u>wants to be a friend of the world makes himself an enemy of God</u>.* Anyone who has completely committed themselves to be friends with the world is in enmity with God, but anyone who desires friendship with the world makes himself an enemy. If anyone then asks if someone can unknowingly be an enemy of God, the truth is yes, simply because all humanity, apart from Christ, is born with the nature of sin, which opposes God.

Some will conclude with this information how having eternal life is still very difficult to obtain just as it may have been for those in the old covenant and this is somewhat true. Anyone who thinks obtaining eternal life is based on works and good deeds will find it to be extremely difficult. The reason the path to eternal life is difficult is because the path to destruction is easy for humanity. If the path to eternal life was easy, a lot more people would walk it. Even Jesus Himself says in Matt 7:13-14: *"Enter by the narrow gate; for wide is the gate and broad is the way that leads to destruction, and there are many who go in by it. Because narrow is the gate and* _difficult is the way which leads to life, and there are few who find it._ In this Text, Jesus makes clear why it is difficult to walk the path to life. The path to the gate of destruction is wide and the path is broad, but the key is when He says, 'there are many who go in by it'. This simply means they willfully choose to go down the path of destruction. Concerning the narrow gate which leads to life, Jesus says 'there are few who find it'. This means while on the broad path, each person must choose not to enter the wide gate and search for the narrow path leading to life. Then they must find it and begin to walk on it until they enter by way of the narrow gate. It is also easy in choosing to walk down the broad path because humanity is already on it and it does not require any work to walk down it. The narrow path however, getting to it will take some work and many are not willing to work for it.

Now, this work everyone must put forth in obtaining life is simply not according to one's own abilities, but the general basis of it all comes down to choices and application through obedience. None of this can happen without the repentance of sins and errors. Repentance has been a call and a gift from God upon man from generation to generation. As many think it to be, repentance is not merely telling God in prayer 'I repent'. God is not concerned with the vociferous who do not apply anything. Liken it unto a violent man who has a repetitive behavior of physically hurting his wife. When he hits her in anger and realizes what he has done, after the fact, by saying 'I'm sorry', then it is a man simply who sees what he does is wrong. If afterwards he hits her again and apologizes again, is he sorry for what he is doing? Now if a man who has never committed this error against his wife, find themselves in a heated argument, and out of a reaction, the man gets so angry he hits her. If this man apologizes for his wrong and never again for the rest of his life lays another hand on her; truly this is a man who is sorry for what he has done. Likewise, in repentance, a man who continues to do the wrong and are aware of it after his many apologies and 'I repent' is like the man in the first example to God. The true example of repentance before God is of the example of the second man. The important factor in this is not how many times the man has errored in his way, but whether he ceases from committing the error. God equally forgives a man who has committed the same error 77 times over, just as much as the man who committed the error once, so long as it is an error he never commits again.

In the fullness of repentance comes a process involving three steps. First, the individual must have their eyes opened in being able to see their ways. Once a person's eyes are opened, they must be able to recognize it to be an erroneous way. Lastly, when an individual recognizes the error of their way, they must turn away from it. The error of man is anything a person does against God's Will and contrary to the commands of the Scriptures. God gives a command, 'do not steal'. If a man is stealing, he is doing what is against God's command. Therefore, the man is in error of his way before God. Turning away from an error is a two-way act which must be done simultaneously. As <u>one empties themself of the desire to do wrong before God</u>, at the same time, must <u>begin to fill themselves with the desire to obey God's command</u>. Too frequently do many in the faith desire and strive to put away carnality but find themselves wrestling with it. The anticipation of such is to be expected for newer believers. It is grieving to see the amount of people who have been professing Christ, as long as they have, still wresting at the magnitude and level of those new to the faith. Being filled with the desires to obey God must come from an individual to know what God commands through the <u>reading of Scriptures</u>, connecting and <u>communing with God through prayer</u>, and with <u>total dependency on the Holy Spirit of God</u>, **not on oneself**, <u>to perform the work</u>. Any individual who repents and ask God for the forgiveness of his/her sins within the works of repentance, and believe in the Son of God, not only in what He suffered, but also being the truth and the way which leads to life, count them to be a part of the few who has <u>begun</u> walking the narrow path.

Repentance is only but the beginning of the journey to salvation. Not only is it the beginning, but it is not a once in a lifetime act. Every day is a day to examine oneself to test if they are still in the faith. In everyday activities and routines, a person, in some form or fashion, will see they committed an act unpleasant to the Lord. It is easy for mankind to focus on the major areas in what God gave in the Ten Commandments, but God is also interested in the details of things anyone may consider less significant. In a life of repentance, an individual is literally being renewed and transformed into the perfect image of His Son in everything. This includes, actions, reactions, speech, attitude, thoughts, and even in the things a person is not even conscious of at times. This is not a matter of saying one prayer and being good for the rest of life to live as one pleases. Just as much work it took to find and walk the narrow path, it is rather very easy to jump back off and walk the broad path again. Ultimately, repentance is a beginning work and process leading to **transformation**[1].

Transformation is such a magnificent and powerful work of God. Nothing outside of God himself has the power or ability to change the internal nature of any creation. Mankind has no power or ability to change its own nature, nor does any idol god humanity has created and worshiped. This is a supernatural work and evidence of God's power and His existence. There are many who question His existence and presence, but the evidence is always in true believers and around everyone. Mankind should not question what truth is, but whether if they have a will to see and acknowledge the truth. Now, transformation is a two-fold process. Transformation literally begins with destroying a previous nature and building a new one. Each individual is being transformed from the rule and subjection of the nature of sin into rule and subjection of the righteousness of God, fulfilled in Christ, and done by the work of the Holy Spirit. Ultimately, transformation cannot be without true repentance and true repentance cannot be without the work of transformation. Anyone who repents will be transformed and anyone experiencing transformation is a result of repentance.

What is in it for humanity in this supernatural work concludes having a change in mind. Paul says best in a very familiar and quoted Text in Romans 12:1-2: *I beseech you therefore, brethren, by the mercies of God, that you present your bodies a living sacrifice, holy, acceptable to God, which is your reasonable service. And <u>do not be conformed to this world, but be transformed by the renewing of your mind</u>, that you may prove what is that good and acceptable and perfect will of God.* This work in its simplest term, is simply having a change of mind. A stealing man decides in his mind, after recognizing the error of his ways, to no longer steal. There will be many times where temptation will be before him to steal just as anyone else will experience temptations. Over time however, in the full work of transformation, it should be easier for the man to say no to the temptation and desire it less. This is evidence of the power of God at work. Anyone who still wrestles with the temptations at a high magnitude over a long period of time is evidence how the working power of transformation is not at work. It is not because God lacks the ability to transform, but because the mind of the individual still desires the sin. This is therefore, one of many evidences of the power of God not being in the person. The Scriptures does say in Rom 8:9 about those without the Holy Spirit when it says: *But you are not in the flesh but in the Spirit, if indeed the Spirit of God dwells in you. **Now if anyone does not have the Spirit of Christ, he is not His***.

Some ask, 'how long is this process of repentance and transformation?' The process begins the day God begins the work in individuals and ends when the person leaves the earth. There is assurance of two things according to the Scriptures when it says in Phil 1:6: *being confident of this very thing, that <u>He who has begun a good work in you will complete it until the day of Jesus Christ</u>,* and in John 10:28-30 where Jesus says: *And I give them eternal life, <u>and they shall never perish; neither **shall anyone snatch them out of My hand**</u>. My Father, who has given them to Me, is greater than all; and **no one is able to snatch them out of My Father's hand**. I and My Father are one."* Any person truly in the hands of God will always remain in God's hands. These individuals see how precious and valuable eternal life is through Christ and will have no desire to turn back to what is temporary and full of empty promises. In 1 John 5:18 the Scriptures says: *We know that <u>everyone who has been born of God does not keep on sinning</u>, but he who was born of God protects him, and the evil one does not touch him.* Some have questioned the fullness of this out of witnessing what appeared to be 'seasoned saints' walk away from the faith completely. Scriptures also testify of this very same picture in 1 John 2:18-19 when it says: *Children, it is the last hour, and as you have heard that antichrist is coming, so now many antichrists have come. Therefore we know that it is the last hour.* <u>*They went out from us, but they were not of us;*</u> **_for if they had been of us, they would have continued with us_**. *But they went out, that it might become plain that they all are not of us.* John even concludes as to the reason why they 'went out from among us.' Hence, it is a prime picture of what it looks like when things hidden in the dark are exposed and come to the light.

A lot has been stated on repentance and transformation, but there is still so much the Scriptures gives considering it. What is provided here is more than enough a foundation to grasp hold of. If anyone is going to see society growing in biblical men, it must begin here. Finally, fellow brothers and sisters in the faith, receive this final exhortation. The time is at hand and as the day comes ever more quickly, let all those who desire eternal life in Christ answer God's call to repent and believe in Jesus Christ. Be reminded everyday with all the events taking place, God is in control of everything. Everything He allows to happen is all for His glory. It is God's reputation on the line, and He will not allow anything to happen which is against His will. God speaks on many occasions, the reason events happen the way they are done, is so everyone 'may know that I am the Lord thy God'. Let every man and woman bow a knee, believe Jesus Christ is the Son of God, receive the mercies of God through the confession of sins through the lips, and praise Him for the extension of His mercy and grace forever and ever, Amen

In-text
References

Page 1.

Dominion – Heb: [radah] pr: raw-daw 7287 – (come to, make to) have dominion, prevail against, reign (bear, make to) rule (rule over), take.

Page 3.

Communion – Heb: [seach] pr: say'-akh 7808 {see 7878 siyach pr: see'-akh} – converse (with oneself, and hence, aloud) or utter: - commune, complain, declare, meditate, muse, pray, speak, talk (with).

Relationship – See communion

Marriage – Heb: [chathunnah] pr: khath-oon-naw 2861 {see 2859 chathan pr: khaw-than} – to give (a daughter) away in marriage; hence, to contract affinity by marriage – join in affinity.

Page 4.

Finds – Heb: [matsa] pr: maw-tsaw 4672 – to come forth to, i.e. appear or exist; to attain, i.e. find or acquire; to occur, meet or be present; be able, befall, being, catch, certainly, (cause to) come (on, to, to hand), deliver, be enough (cause to) find (-ing, occasion, out), get (hold upon), have (there), be here, be left, light (up-) on, meet (with), occasion serve, (be) present, ready, speed, suffice, take hold on.

Temptation – Heb: [maccha] pr: mas-saw 4531 – a testing, of men (judicial) or of God (querulous) – temptation, trial {see 5254 nacah pr: naw-saw} – to test, to attempt; adventure, assay, prove, tempt, try.

Page 5

Family – Heb: [mishpachah] pr: mish-paw-khaw 4940 – circle of relatives; a class (of persons), a species (of animals or sort (of things); a tribe of people; - family, kind (-red).

State – Heb: [nuwach] pr: noo-ack 5117– to rest, i.e. settle down; used in a great variety of applications, (to dwell, stay, let fall, place, let alone, withdraw, give comfort, etc); - cease, be confederate, lay, let down, (be) quiet, remain, (cause to, be at, give, have, make to) rest, set down.

Page 6

Church – Gr: [ekklesia] pr: ek-klay-see-ah 1577 – a popular meeting, espec. A religious congregation (Jewish synagogue, or Chr. Community of members on earth or saints in heave or both): - assembly, church.

Page 8

Sin – Heb: [chatta'ah or chatta'th] pr: khat-taw-aw or khat-tawth 2403 – an offence (sometimes habitual sinfulness), and its penalty, occasion, sacrifice, or expiation; also an offender; - punishment (of sin), purifying (-fication for sin), sin (-ner, offering).

Page 10

Transgression – Heb: [pesha'] pr: peh-shah 6588 – a revolt (national, moral, or religious): - rebellion, sin, transgression, trespass {see 6586 pasha' pr: paw-shah} – to break away (from just authority), i.e. trespass, apostatize, quarrel: - offend, rebel, revolt, transgress (-ion, -or).

Page 17

Prosperity – See prosper

Page 18

Prosper – Gr: [euodoo] pr: yoo-od-o-o 2137 – to help on the road, i.e. (pass.) succeed in reaching; fig. to succeed in business affairs: - (have a) prosper (-ous journey).

Prospered – See prosper
Prospers – See prosper
Prosperous – See prosper
Fornicator – Heb: [zanah] pr: zaw-naw 2181 – to commit adultery (usually of the female, and less often of simple fornication, rarely of involuntary ravishment); fig. to commit idolatry (the Jewish people being regarded as the spouse of Jehovah): - (cause to) commit fornication, continually, great, (be an, play the) harlot, (cause to be, play the) whore, (commit, fall to) whoredom, (cause to) go a-whoring, whorish.

Profane – Heb: [chalal] pr: khaw-lal 2490 – to bore, i.e. (by impl.) to wound, to dissolve; fig. to profane (a person, place, or thing), to break (one's word), break: - profane (self), prostitute, slay (slain), sorrow, stain, wound.

Repentance – Heb: [nacham] pr: naw-kham 5162 – to sigh, i.e. breathe strongly; by impl. To be sorry, i.e. (in a favorable sense), to pity, console; or (unfavorably) to avenge (oneself).

Page 19

Hate – Heb: [sane] pr: saw-nay 8130 – to hate (personally): - enemy, foe, (be) hate (-ful, -r), odious.

Abhors – Heb: [ta'ab] pr: taw-ab 8581 – to loathe, i.e. (mor) detest, - (make to be) abhor (-red), (be, commit more, do) abominable (-y).

Page 29

Helper – Heb: [ezer] pr: ay-zer 5828 – aid–help

Comparable – Heb: [neged] pr: neh-ghed 5048 – part opposite; spec. a counterpart, or mate; usually (adv., espec. With prep.) over against or before.

Page 31

Myriad – Heb [ribbow] pr: rib-bo 7239 – a myriad, i.e. indef. large number; - great things. {Substituted with ten thousand.}

Page 35

Silence – Gr: [hesuchia] pr: hay-soo-khee-ah 2271 – stillness, i.e. desistance from bustle or language: - quietness, silence. {see also 4601 sigao pr: see-gah-o} – to keep silent (tran. Or intr.): - keep close (secret, silence), hold peace.

Page 37

Admonish – Gr: [noutheteo] pr: noo-thet-eh'-o 3560 – to put in mind, i.e. (by impl.) to caution or reprove gently; - admonish, warn.

Page 40

Hallowed – Heb: [qadash] pr: kaw-dash 6942 – to be (caus. Make, pronounce or observe as) clean (cerem. Or mor.): - appoint, bid, consecrate, dedicate, defile, hallow, (be, keep) holy (-er, place), keep, prepare, proclaim, purify, sanctify (ied one, self), wholly. – (substituted with consecrated)

Page 47

Born again – Gr: [anagennao] pr: an-ag-en-nah-o 313 – to beget or (by extens,) bear (again): - beget, (bear again).

Page 49

Spitefully – Gr: [hubrizo] pr: hoo-brid-zo 5195 – to exercise violence, i.e. abuse: - use despitefully, reproach, entreat shamefully (spitefully)

Page 52

Enmity – Heb: [Ebah] pr: ay-baw 342 – hostility: - enmity, hatred.

Page 56

Transformation – Gr: [metamorphoo] pr: met-am-or-fo-o 3339 – to transform (lit. or fig. "metamorphose"): - change, transfigure, transform.

Alley Katt

Volume One: JOY

A Novel

by

Derrick A. Bonner

Dedicated to all the strong women who stand beside as well as have their men's backs. If it weren't for you, we men would never survive our stories, and we'd never get our happily ever after's.